# RAVEL

## SONATINE FOR THE PIANO

EDITED BY MAURICE HINSON

AN ALFRED MASTERWORK EDITION

Second Edition
Copyright © MMII by Alfred Publishing Co., Inc.
All rights reserved. Printed in USA.
ISBN 0-7390-1056-5

*Cover art:* Argenteuil, *1875*
*by Claude Monet (1840–1926)*
*Orangerie, Paris*
© Giraudon / Art Resource, NY

*This edition is dedicated to my dear friend
and colleague James Bonn, with much appreciation and admiration.*

# PREFACE

The first movement of the *Sonatine* was completed in 1903 and entered in a competition sponsored by the *Weekly Critical Review*. Soon after, however, the contest was canceled as the periodical quickly approached financial collapse. Two years later the work was completed with the addition of the second and third movements. Paule de Lestang gave the world premiere of this work on March 10, 1906.

The modest title *Sonatine* conceals an elaborate composition that is full of gossamer grace and represents Ravel's neo-classicism at its best. This work is cyclical and uses thematic material based on the interval of the perfect fourth and its inversion, the perfect fifth. Ravel was meticulous in specifying dynamics, phrasing, and tempo changes, but was less precise about pedaling and he indicated no fingerings. He also made numerous passages unnecessarily difficult to play by assigning too many notes to one hand; redistributing the notes between the left and right hands makes the task considerably easier. With this idea in mind, I have suggested some redistributions.

The first movement *(Modéré)* is in F sharp minor (natural minor) which is a transposition of the Aeolian mode and is in *sonata-allegro* form. The first theme is heard in measures 1–12: use very little pedal in this opening section; the short second theme is stated in measures 13–19; a transition leads to a repeat of the exposition (first ending), and then to the development (second ending). The development section covers measures $26^2$ to 55. The first theme is developed in measures $26^2$ to 39; focus on the second theme occurs in measures 40–55. The recapitulation from measures 56 to 84 is a repetition of the exposition with appropriate key changes.

Ravel's recommendation regarding this movement was "to avoid emphasizing the rhythm; the theme would become vulgar." This movement is generally played too fast. Ravel has indicated *Modéré*, so even in its most passionate outbursts, it still requires an aristocratic restraint. The tiny break between the two statements of the first theme (measure 3) is essential. Clarify the shape of the three layers of sonority in the opening bars (1–9). In measure 2, note that the A in the left hand beginning the second beat is taken by the right hand. Use the same distribution in the first of measure 5 and all similar passages. At measure 81, the right hand should be supported by much arm weight in its search for depth of expression. Follow carefully Ravel's phrasing with regard to upbeat beginnings. Some examples are the F sharp at the end of measure 5 and the B at the end of measure 33.

The enchanting second movement *(Mouvement de menuet)* in D flat major displays a typical minuet rhythm with the accented or prolonged note on the second beat. This movement bears a spiritual affinity with Prokofiev's *Classical Symphony:* both are modal, antique, and utterly delightful. The traditional trio is missing. The form is sectional and might be described as rondo-like: A B C A B. A: bars 1–12 and repeated—all the motifs are present in various guises. Implement Ravel's phrasing slurs carefully in these first 12 bars. B: bars 13–33—romantic and impressionistic harmony tinged with whole-tone color (bar 14). C: bars 33–52 serve as a linking passage that could be thought of as taking the place occupied by a trio in a more traditional movement. At measures 39–45 there is a brief reference to the opening theme of the first movement. The left hand arpeggio chords in these measures should come out like a harp effect. A: bars 53–64, modified to end in the tonic. B: bars 65–82, with coda from bar 78 to the end, modified to center on the tonic. Use the sostenuto pedal to catch the bass grace notes D flat and A flat at the end of measure 80. Be careful of too much pedal in this tender and nostalgically graceful movement. The harmonies must not sound thick.

The third movement *(Animé)* is brilliant, very dashing, toccata-like, and is written in *sonata-allegro* form. Introduction: bars 1–3, modal opening with Dorian mode transposed. Exposition: (A) bars 4–36, (B) bars 37–53; Codetta: bars 54–59. Development: bars 60–105. Recapitulation: (A) bars 106–139, (B) bars 140–156. Coda: bars 157 to the end. Begin measure 165 less strongly in order to bring out the *crescendo* effectively.

This movement requires rapid changes of position, considerable power, and a well-developed sense of key balance for its repeated notes. Special attention is directed to measures 37–39. Many players ignore the direction *Même mouvement tranquille* because they regard the section as a passage *leading back* to the opening theme of the first movement. In reality, it *leads towards and into* that theme, and adherence to Ravel's direction provides a perfectly convincing result. Be aware of the counterrhythms in measures 47–52 where the bass line is in 3/4 whereas the melody is underlaid with a 2/4 pulse.

Numerous single upbeat right hand sixteenth notes permeate the movement, and these must be clearly heard since they are pertinent to the melodic line. The difficulty arises because these sixteenths are so often directly preceded by the very same note in the left hand, so when this movement is played up to tempo the right hand sixteenth is frequently missed. By playing the left hand note staccato, the same note in the right hand can be heard clearly. I have indicated some of these places with the reminder "staccato."

*Sonatine* lasts ca. 11 minutes and is one of the most tightly organized and classically oriented works to come from Ravel's pen.

**Maurice Hinson**

## Maurice Ravel
(1875–1937)

*Illustration: Cheryl Thornburg*

Maurice Ravel at the piano in 1912 (Roland-Manuel).

Ravel in his study at Montfort-l'Amaury in 1933 (Lipnitzki).

# Sonatine

## I

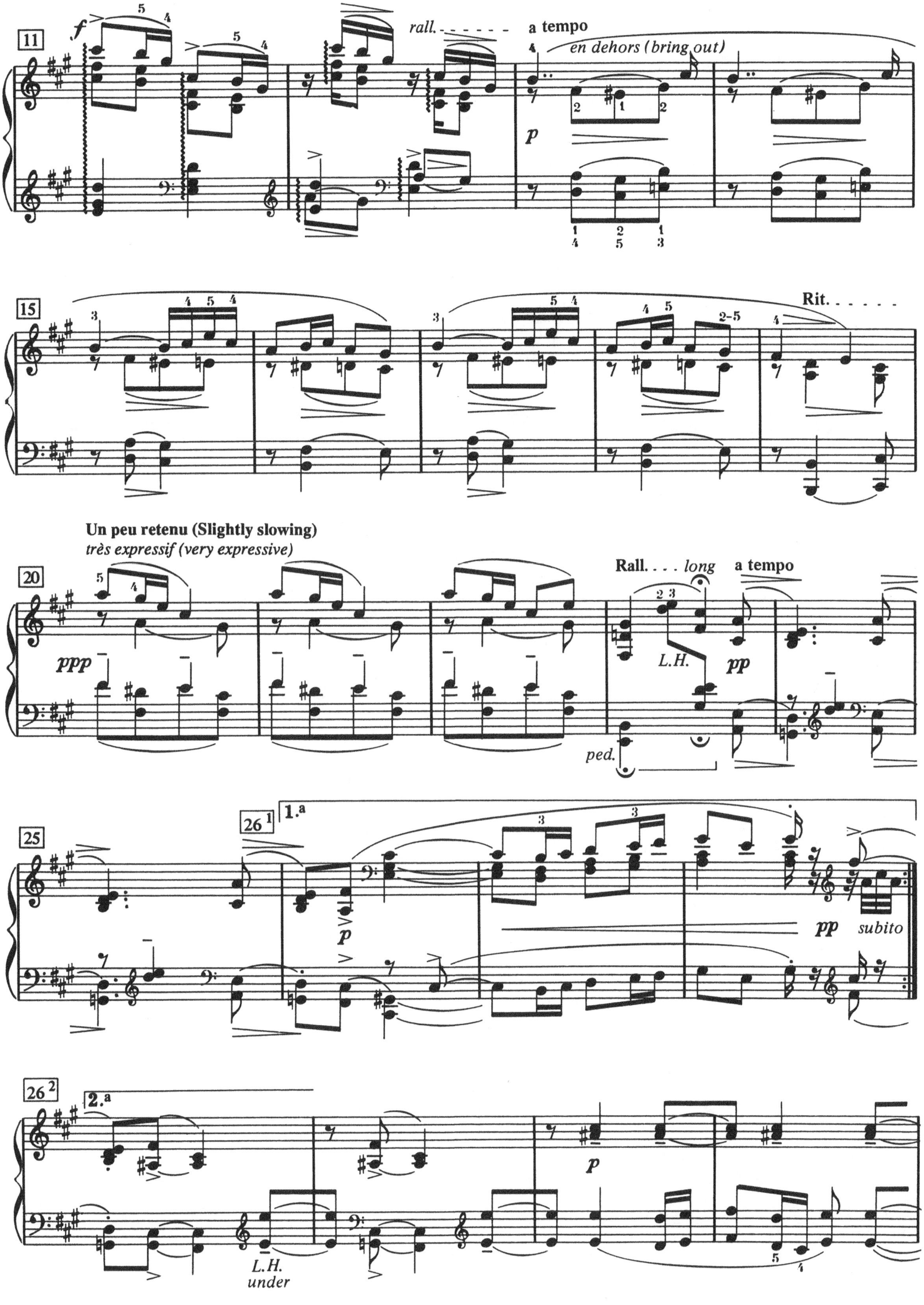
11
f
rall.
a tempo
en dehors (bring out)
p
15
Rit.
Un peu retenu (Slightly slowing)
très expressif (very expressive)
20
ppp
Rall. . . . long
a tempo
L.H.
pp
ped.
25
26 1
1.a
p
pp
subito
26 2
2.a
p
L.H.
under

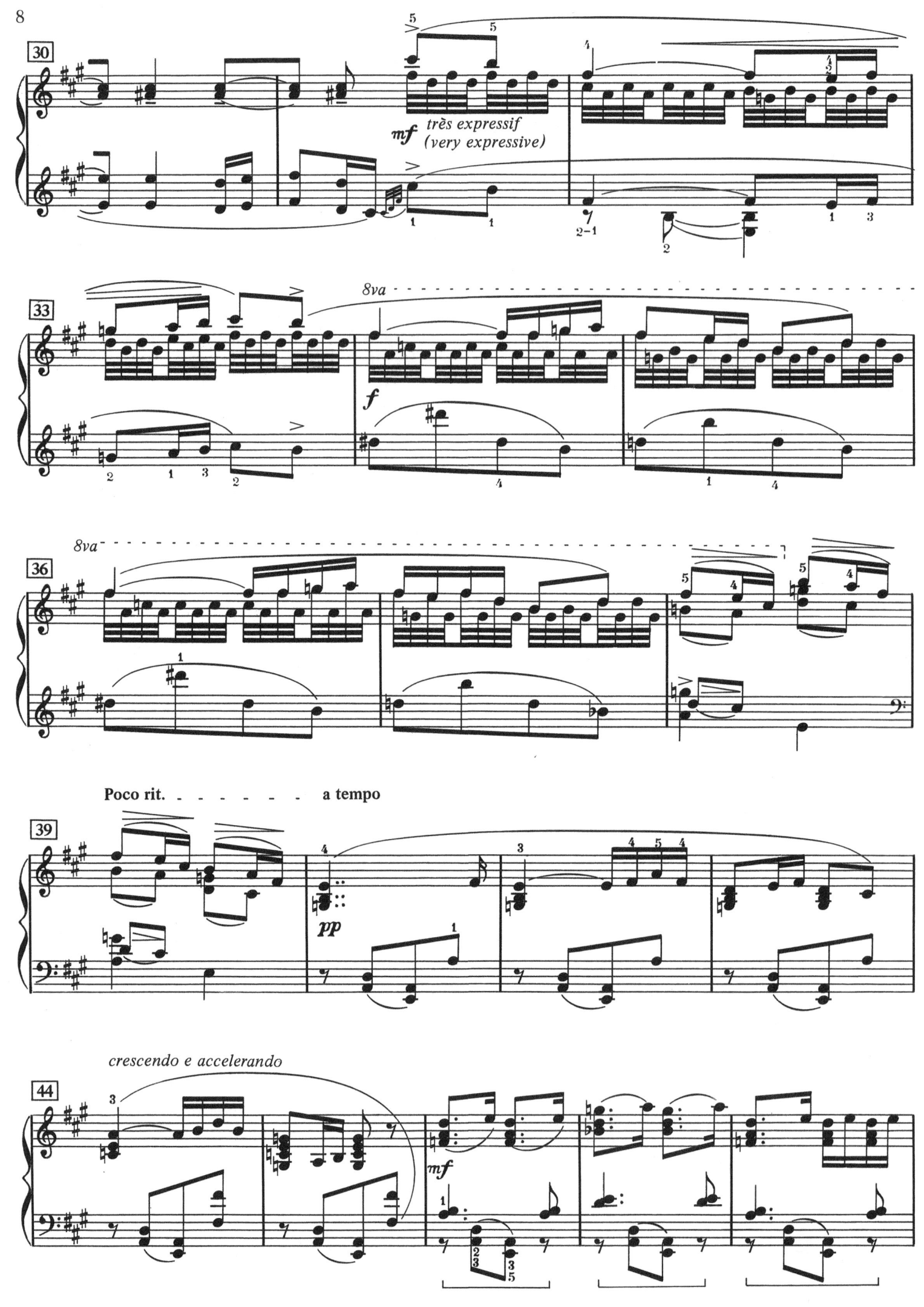

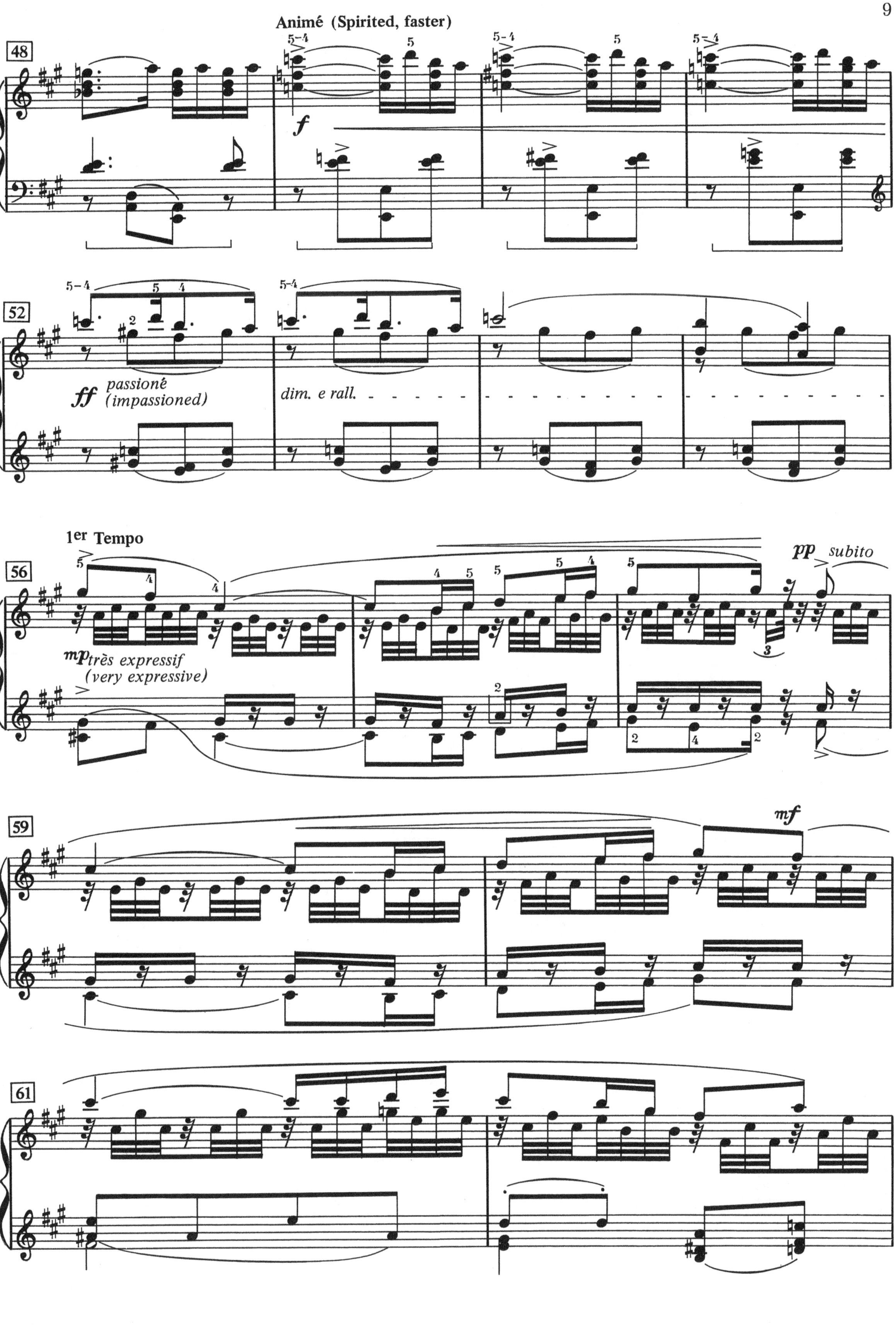
Animé (Spirited, faster)
48
f
52
ff passioné
(impassioned)
dim. e rall.
1er Tempo
56
mp très expressif
(very expressive)
pp subito
59
mf
61

# II

**27**

*ppp*
*en dehors (bring out)*

*p*

**33**
*8va - - - - -*         Rall.

*f*      *ff*

**(Slower)**
**Plus lent** *8va - - - - - - -*
**39** *pp*

*p* *en dehors et expressif*
*(bring out and expressive)*

**(Gradually returning to the first tempo)**
**Reprenez peu à peu le Mouvement**          a tempo

**45**

*pp*

**(With no ritard)**
**Sans ralentir**

**51**

# III

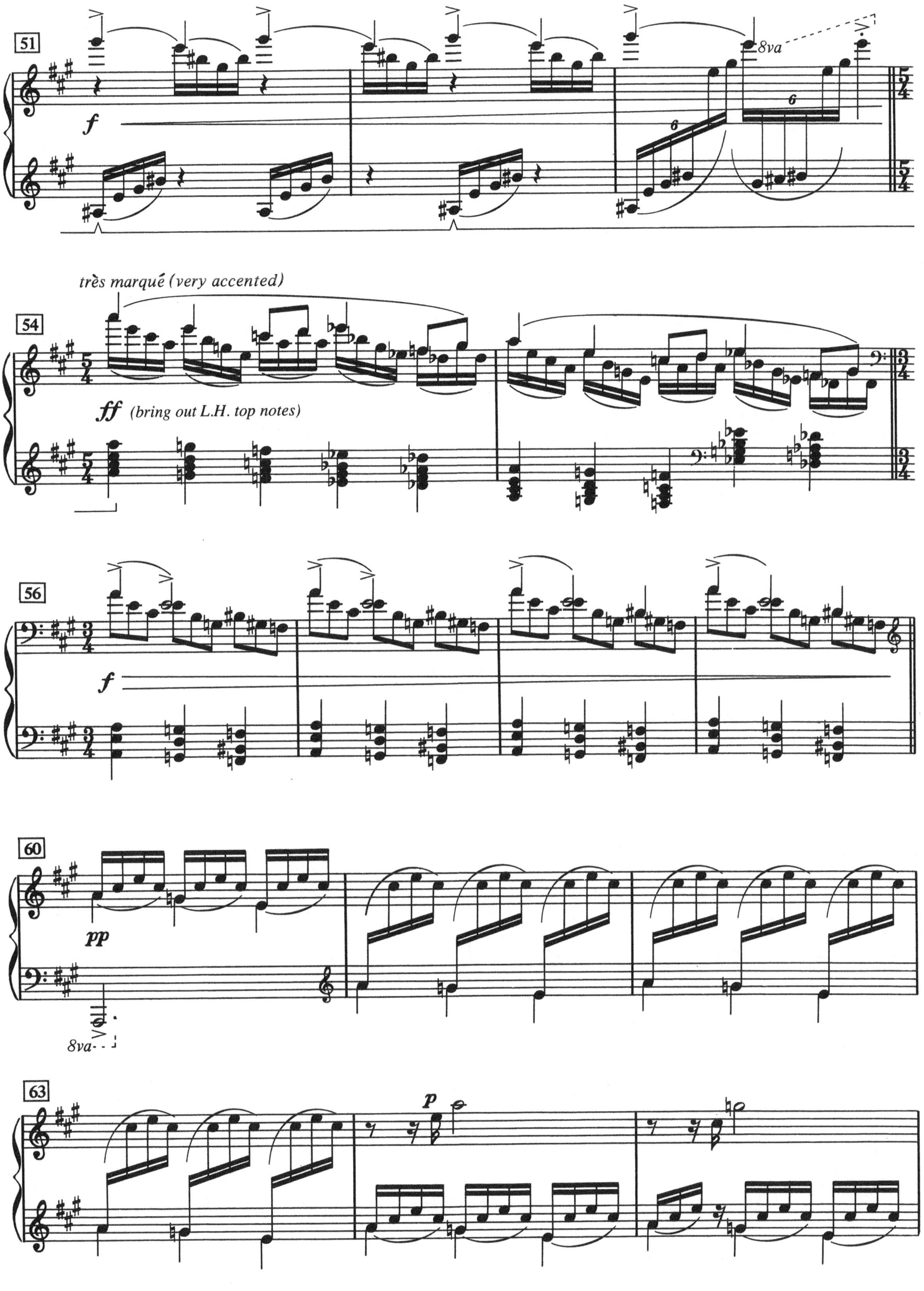
51
f
6
6
8va
54
très marqué (very accented)
ff (bring out L.H. top notes)
56
f
60
pp
8va
63
p

pp marqué
(accented)

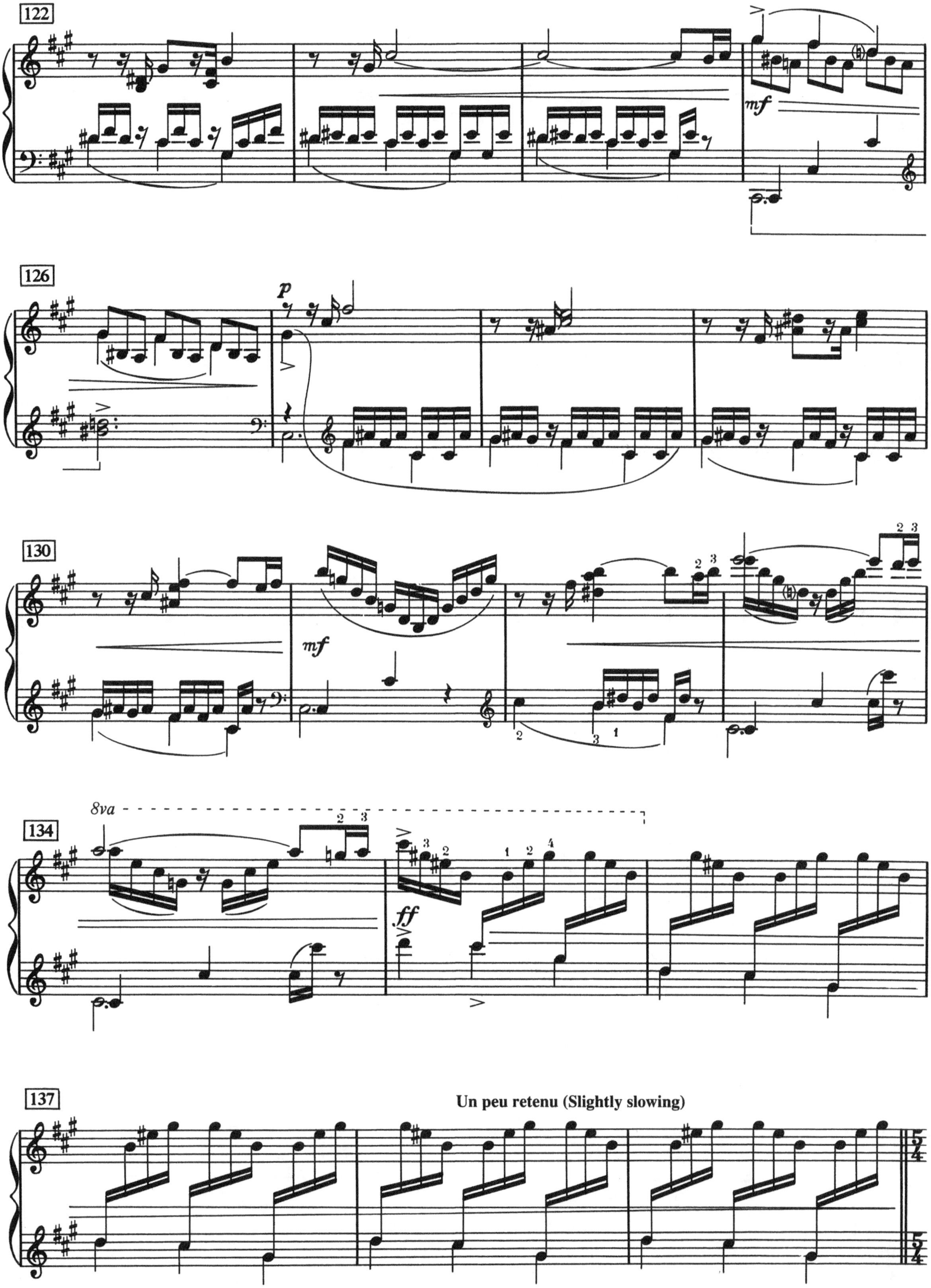
122
mf
126
p
130
mf
8va
134
ff
137
Un peu retenu (Slightly slowing)

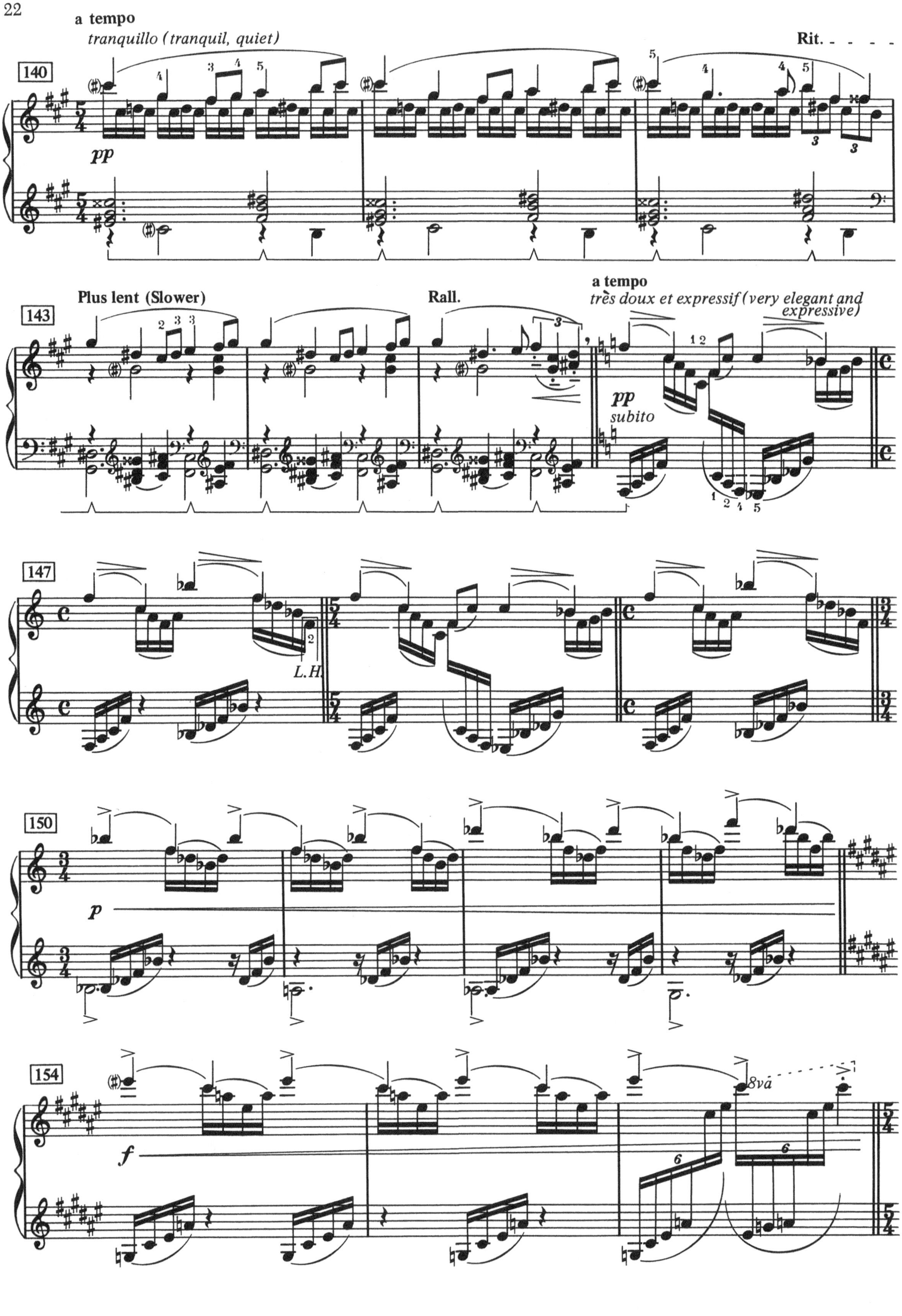
a tempo
tranquillo (tranquil, quiet)
Rit. - - - - -
140
pp
143
Plus lent (Slower)
Rall.
a tempo
très doux et expressif (very elegant and expressive)
pp
subito
147
L.H.
150
p
154
f
8va